FEDERAL
ACCOUNTING STANDARDS
ADVISORY BOARD

Annual Report
Fiscal Year Ended September 30, 2013

Three-Year Plan
Fiscal Years 2014-2016

Comments Requested by January 31, 2014

Members

Tom Allen, Chairman

Robert Dacey, Government Accountability Office

Norman Dong, Office of Management and Budget

Michael Granof

Sam McCall

Mark Reger, Department of the Treasury

D. Scott Showalter

Graylin Smith

Harold Steinberg

Organization

The Federal Accounting Standards Advisory Board ("FASAB" or "the board") was established in October, 1990, by three federal officials responsible for federal financial reporting—the Secretary of the Treasury, the Director of the Office of Management and Budget, and the Comptroller General of the United States. These three officials possess legal authority under various laws to establish accounting and financial reporting standards for the federal government. Together, they entered into and have periodically modified a memorandum of understanding creating the board as a federal advisory committee.

Membership comprises individuals from each of the three federal agencies that established the board ("the sponsors") and six non-federal individuals.

Mission

The FASAB serves the public interest by improving federal financial reporting through issuing federal financial accounting standards and providing guidance after considering the needs of external and internal users of federal financial information.

The Mission Supports Public Accountability

Financial reports, which include financial statements prepared in conformity with generally accepted accounting principles, are essential for public accountability and for an efficient and effective functioning of our democratic system of government. Thus, the board plays a major role in fulfilling the government's responsibility to be publicly accountable. Federal financial reports should be useful in assessing (1) the government's accountability and its efficiency and effectiveness, and (2) the economic, political, and social consequences, whether positive or negative, of the allocation and various uses of federal resources.

TABLE OF CONTENTS

Annual Report

From the Chairperson

Meeting its mission while making the best use of resources is a challenge faced by every federal organization and FASAB is no exception. We strive both to ensure the public can assess how well taxpayer resources are used and to use our resources effectively. During fiscal year (FY) 2013, the board took the following significant actions to improve its strategic focus, outreach, and effectiveness:

- Issued the FY 2012 annual report and three-year plan as a joint report by November 15, 2012, so that stakeholder input was available when we set our priorities.

- Carefully weighed input received and established our priorities for FY 2014 – 2016 early in the fiscal year.

- Developed objectives and strategies for outreach to members of Congress and their staff to encourage Congressional input regarding our proposals.

- Planned to collaborate with the Governmental Accounting Standards Board (GASB) in a project to enhance lease accounting standards.

- Consulted with the Financial Accounting Standards Board's (FASB) staff regarding their modifications to insurance accounting standards and service concession arrangements.

- Leveraged our resources by recruiting a working group to independently research issues raised regarding accounting for internal use software and develop a proposal for resolving those issues.

- Continued active interaction with task forces on each active project and the broader financial management and audit communities.

As we plan for future activities, your input regarding our updated three-year plan – which also identifies potential projects not prioritized for action during the next three-years – is needed. We have included the three-year plan in this report beginning at page 10. We encourage you to provide feedback on the plan so that we can consider your views during our review of the plan in February 2014.

We hope this annual report and three-year plan helps our stakeholders monitor our standards-setting process and progress, assess how well we performed against the American Institute of CPAs (AICPA) criteria for generally accepted accounting principles (GAAP) standards-setting bodies, and offer suggestions to us. Your input regarding the content of this report is welcome. Please send your comments to *fasab@fasab.gov*.

> *The* Federal government has a fundamental responsibility to be effective stewards of taxpayer dollars.
>
> We must be responsible with money that comes in to the government, money that is spent, and money that is used in running the government itself.
>
> Decision makers and the public must have confidence that the government is managing its finances effectively to minimize inefficient and wasteful spending, to make informed decisions about managing government programs, and to implement policy.
>
> Finance.Performance.gov
> (August 1, 2013)

Board Technical Activities

Completed Standards

During the fiscal year, the board issued standards:

- guiding entities to report the effects of impairments to general property, plant and equipment (G-PP&E) when they occur. Upon implementation in FY 2015, users of financial statements will be able to discern the cost of **impairments** when they occur, the financial impact on the reporting entity, and the cost of services provided following the impairment. The standards provide a cost-effective approach in light of the diverse universe of federal G-PP&E.

- allowing an additional year for auditors to prepare needed audit guidance regarding **long-term fiscal projections.** In FY 2014, without further Board action, information about the present value of projected receipts and non-interest spending under current policy without change will be presented as a basic financial statement. This will allow users of the consolidated financial statements to assess "whether future budgetary resources will likely be sufficient to sustain public services and to meet obligations as they come due." [1]

> ### IMPROVING COST, BUDGET, AND PERFORMANCE INFORMATION
>
> **1967...**
>
> "Interrelationships between appropriations and obligations, and between obligations and costs, are worthy of careful examination. Appropriations..are and will continue to be the important first step in the expenditure process. ...Recording of obligations is essential for financial control and accountability of agency appropriations. Obligations are, however, increasingly recognized as generally inadequate for measurement of agency performance and are being replaced by program costs for this purpose as rapidly as development of adequate accounting systems permits."
>
> Report of the President's Commission on Budget Concepts – October 1967
>
> **2013...**
>
> "...to shift the conversation and look through a different lens around cost is something industry does every day, but government doesn't necessarily do. So, frankly it's an industry best practice we are trying to bring in."
>
> Beth McGrath, Deputy Chief Management Officer, DoD (as quoted in *Federal News*)

Ongoing and New Projects

The board issued for public comment its proposed standards regarding the **federal reporting entity** in April 2013. Development of standards addressing the complex relationships established by the federal government will help ensure financial reports cover the organizations for which elected officials are accountable. Existing concepts provide rules that exclude specific organizations. The board has proposed principles rather than rules regarding organizations such as the Federal Reserve and "bailout" entities excluded under current concepts. The proposal addresses principles that guide preparers of financial statements in determining what organizations should be included in federal financial reports as well as how to present information about organizations. A public hearing was held in August 2013 and the Board hopes to finalize standards in FY 2014.

The **reporting model** project objective is to ensure the information available—both through the general purpose federal financial reports themselves and the systems that support the reports—is relevant and understandable to users. The board identified user needs after extensive outreach to various types of users and solicited recommendations from two task forces as well as roundtable participants. Based on this extensive research, the board decided to focus on improving performance reporting, the statement of net cost, and budgetary information. Task forces on each topic were asked to develop actionable ideas for the board's consideration.

---

[1] Statement of Federal Financial Accounting Concepts (SFFAC) 1, paragraphs 135 and 139.

During FY 2013, the task forces on *cost, budget, and performance information* recommended revisiting managerial cost accounting standards to help provide the cost information that users expect and help the federal government better manage its costs. Because the recommended project is broad and involves matters that are not exclusively within the board's purview, coordination with our sponsors will be fundamental to any cost accounting effort the Board decides to initiate. Specific actions considered include integrating budget, cost, and service performance information; revisiting managerial cost accounting standards; disaggregating cost information; distinguishing transfer payments from program administrative costs; and clarifying conceptual guidance on displaying costs.

The board determined that a model of the ideal presentation is needed to guide such efforts. A conceptual model that integrates budget, cost, and service performance information is being developed with the recognition that financial statements and other information consistent with the model cannot be accomplished immediately. The ideal model is being developed with an awareness that some aspects may require policy and/or systems changes that may not be possible for many years. For example, meeting the desire for information on the cost of programs rather than more highly aggregated costs, such as by goal or by organization, may require policies and systems that support cost analysis. After developing the ideal model, the board will need to identify specific projects so that manageable segments are addressed in the best order.

The staff is working closely with a task force to identify issues regarding accounting for **public-private partnerships** (P3s). P3s are increasingly being used to provide needed government services. The challenge is to be able to measure the cost of partnerships and reveal the underlying risks. This should enable users to compare the cost of such partnerships to the cost of other delivery mechanisms. During FY 2013, the board considered proposed definitions and risk disclosures. Recognition and measurement guidance will be coordinated with related projects such as leases and reporting entity.

The board is also addressing **risk assumed** because existing risk assumed requirements apply only to insurance contracts and explicit guarantees of transactions other than loans (hereafter "non-loan guarantees"). Reporting on all significant risks assumed, not just risks related to insurance contracts and non-loan guarantees, is important to meeting federal financial reporting objectives. Further, there is inconsistency in the presentation of risk assumed information for insurance contracts and non-loan guarantees. The first phase of the project is focusing on insurance and non-loan guarantee programs. A proposal will be drafted in FY 2014.

Current standards for **leases** are viewed by some as not making meaningful distinctions between capital and operating leases. Significant changes have been proposed to private sector standards for lease accounting. The board is collaborating with the GASB so that experiences and ideas, where appropriate, can be shared and common solutions developed.

Implementation Guidance

Implementation guidance was provided to federal agencies through the Accounting and Auditing Policy Committee (AAPC). The AAPC is a committee comprising representatives from the Chief Financial Officers Council, the Council of Inspectors General on Integrity and Efficiency, the U. S. Department of the Treasury ("Treasury"), the Office of Management and Budget (OMB), and the U. S. Government Accountability Office (GAO). The board's executive director serves as chairperson of the committee. While the board provides staff support, the committee accomplishes its mission largely through the efforts of volunteers serving on task forces. Volunteers come from federal agencies, independent public accounting firms, and nonprofit organizations. The committee is currently seeking to resolve long-standing issues related to accounting for PP&E. During the year, the AAPC completed guidance for identifying the costs incurred to place G-PP&E into service.

Collaboration

The board continues to work collaboratively with other standards-setting boards including the GASB, the board that establishes accounting and financial reporting standards for state and local governmental entities in the United States; the FASB, the Board that establishes accounting and financial reporting standards for non-governmental entities in the Unites States; and the International Public Sector Accounting Standards Board (IPSASB), the board that establishes international accounting and financial reporting standards for governmental entities. Generally, such collaboration is at the staff level. However, the project on leases is a collaborative project for which the board anticipates annual joint meetings with GASB to allow members to exchange ideas.

Presentations and Other Assistance

The board and its staff continue to actively support the federal financial management community by providing education, facilitating collaboration among agencies, presenting information and ideas in journal articles, and assisting others. Over 35 hours of educational training were provided by members and staff through their participation in international, national, regional and local conferences sponsored by groups such as the AICPA, AGA, state CPA societies, and the American Accounting Association.

Staff continued to offer its annual update that provides four hours of continuing professional education free of charge to over 70 individuals. In addition, staff members routinely provide assistance to accounting textbook authors and respond to questions regarding federal accounting.

Closing

The board's accomplishments were many this year and we hope to continue to contribute to improving federal governmental transparency and accountability.

The Steering Committee is composed of the chairman and the members representing our sponsors. The committee annually reviews the operating budget, approves contracting activities, and provides the executive director's annual performance appraisal and expectations. The committee also participates actively in the Appointments Panel.

The Appointments Panel, established in 1999, assists the board's sponsors in recruiting and selecting non-federal members and advises the board regarding improvement efforts. The panel comprises the members of the Steering Committee, two representatives of the AICPA, and one representative of the Financial Accounting Foundation (FAF). The panel's assistance contributes greatly to the board's independence and continued conformance to the criteria for a GAAP standards-setting body. The panel assists in preparing this annual report and monitors annual performance survey results. The panel would convey any concerns to the AICPA in a timely manner.

Appointments Panel Members
Tom Allen, Chairman
Robert Dacey, GAO
Norman Dong, OMB
Cynthia Eisenhauer, FAF
F. Carter Heim, AICPA
Harold Monk, AICPA
Mark Reger, Treasury

FASAB General Counsel
Jacquelyn Hamilton

FASAB Executive Director and Designated Federal Official
Wendy Payne

Governance and Operations

Governance Activities

The board did not revise its mission statement (adopted in 2012) or its rules of procedure (adopted in 2010) during FY 2013.

The Steering Committee members continued to emphasize the budget constraints faced by all federal agencies, including their own, but nevertheless affirmed their commitment to supporting the needs of the board. During the year, an additional experienced staff member resigned and brought to two the number of staff vacancies. To mitigate the effect of these losses on the technical agenda, the committee approved:

- filling the FY 2012 staff vacancy at the assistant director level,
- creating an analyst level staff position in FY 2014, and
- contracting for a study regarding managerial cost accounting to serve as a basis for a new project when staff becomes available.

Budgetary resources are reported on page 9. Final FY 2014 resources are dependent upon appropriations established through the federal legislative process. The committee also provided the executive director's annual performance appraisal and established expectations.

The Appointments Panel, in addition to its routine support to the Steering Committee, provided recommendations to the sponsors regarding members whose first terms are expiring next year and established a timeline for future needed appointment actions.

FASAB general counsel, Jacquelyn Hamilton, provided members with training on requirements of the Federal Advisory Committee Act. Such training is helpful to remind members of due process requirements and will be repeated on a regular basis.

Operations

Performance Results

Members confirm their **independence** and adherence to the ethics policy, and complete a board performance survey in an annual assessment of conformance to the five criteria essential for a GAAP standards-setting body. Through the

---

AICPA Criteria for a GAAP Standards-Setting Body

Independence: The body should be independent from the undue influence of its constituency.

Due Process and Standards: The body should follow a due process that is documented and open to all relevant aspects or alternatives. The body's aim should be to produce standards that are timely and that provide for full, fair, and comparable disclosure.

Domain and Authority: The body should have a unique constituency not served by another existing Rule 203 standards-setting body. Its standards should be generally accepted by its constituencies.

Human and Financial Resources: The body should have sufficient funds to support its work. Its members and staff should be highly knowledgeable in all relevant areas.

Comprehensiveness and Consistency: The body should approach its processes comprehensively and follow concepts consistent with those of existing Rule 203 standards-setting bodies for analogous circumstances.

---

survey, each member identifies changes – positive or negative – in the board's performance relative to the five criteria (see sidebar listing of criteria). Members are encouraged to explain their views as well as offer suggestions for improvement. Members consider all views and suggestions during the development of the annual report. This annual report summarizes the consensus results so that member views are made publicly available on a timely basis.

In addition to these annual processes, members agree the AICPA will be notified of any reportable events of undue influence if and when they occur. Together, these efforts serve to alert the AICPA to significant changes relevant to the established criteria and ongoing recognition as the GAAP standards-setting body for federal governmental entities. To date, no reportable events have occurred. Again, this year all members confirmed they conformed to the requirements regarding **independence**, ethics, and reporting undue influence.

Together, these efforts serve to alert the AICPA to significant changes relevant to the established criteria and ongoing recognition as the GAAP standards-setting body for federal governmental entities. To date, no reportable events have occurred. Again, this year all members confirmed they conformed to the requirements regarding independence, ethics, and reporting undue influence.

Further, the survey results show no significant changes during the year but some concern regarding staff turnover and future resources. As noted in Chart 1 on the next page, the majority of members believe there was no change when considering: (1) **due process and standards,** (2) **knowledge of staff and members** (a component of **human resources**), and (3) **comprehensiveness and consistency.**

ANNUAL CONFIRMATION PROVIDED BY MEMBERS

Independence: I acknowledge that I have neither personal nor external impairments that will keep me from objectively reaching independent conclusions on matters under consideration by FASAB, nor did I during the preceding fiscal year. I will promptly notify the Chairperson if my independence is or may be impaired.

Ethics: I have reviewed the FASAB ethics policy and confirm that I satisfied all requirements and limitations established under the policy during the preceding fiscal year.

Undue Influence: I have notified the Chairperson of any and all matters that I judge to be undue influence. "Undue influence" is defined as external influences or pressures that impact a member's ability to objectively reach and/or communicate independent conclusions.

The member noting decline in the "knowledge of members and staff" criteria attributed this change to the loss of another experienced staff member during the year. Resources are discussed further below. Two members reporting a decline in due process suggested more timely delivery of briefing and other materials, more meeting time, providing sufficient time for careful board reviews and responses, and less time spent revisiting issues. The board is addressing these concerns by:

- improving delivery methods for briefing materials (reinstituting Saturday delivery for non-federal members and improving electronic delivery).

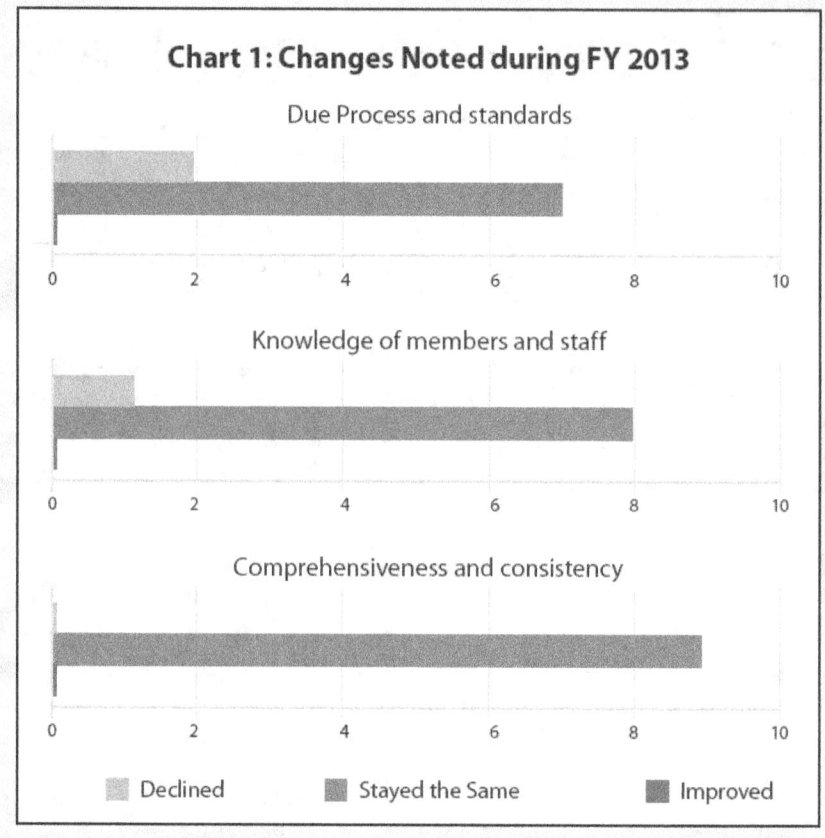

Chart 1: Changes Noted during FY 2013

- relying on task forces and others to brief the members directly regarding key issues.

For the remaining two criteria (**domain and authority**, and **financial resources**), the survey solicits narrative responses. This facilitates identification of ideas for improvement. Improvement efforts begun in FY 2012 have been successful. The board has adopted an annual cycle for reviewing its technical agenda and publishes its three-year plan with this annual report. In FY 2014, the board will augment its efforts to obtain input on the technical agenda by inviting key stakeholders to meet with the board as it begins its annual review.

Members expressed concerns regarding resources both for the current fiscal year and in the future (see the resources section below for detailed information about resources). Some members noted that active projects were delayed by the two staff vacancies and that the priority projects identified in the technical agenda for the upcoming three-year period were important but not able to be addressed. Members expressing these concerns noted:

- the significance and complexity of current projects are high and will require extensive research
- the smaller staff size has translated into slower progress on issues
- the timing of deliberations on new projects, once every two months, slows progress on priority projects
- the board's collective capacity is not being well used as evidenced by the reduction in meeting time due to staff vacancies

One member noted that even with all staff positions filled, the board operates with the minimum staff necessary to address its agenda.

Swift replacement of departing staff is essential to the board's ability to address federal financial reporting issues in a timely manner. As of year end, the assistant director vacancy was filled and planning was underway to fill the second vacancy. Members noted that filling the second vacancy requires that funding uncertainties be resolved favorably. Funding issues were not resolved prior to publication of this annual report.

Some members noted that the void created by staff vacancies was adequately addressed this year by increasing the use of task forces, acquiring contract support, and collaborating with GASB. The board agrees that these efforts to leverage resources should continue.

Other concerns expressed by members include:

- identification of misinterpretations, reporting errors, and implementation challenges with existing standards would be helpful in assessing their clarity and practicality
- the importance of the Congressional outreach efforts agreed to during the year
- more attention is needed on international public sector standards but resources are not available
- the need for regular updates regarding GASB developments

To address these concerns, the board will receive periodic reports from staff regarding technical inquiries, seek input from the audit community, and monitor staff progress on Congressional outreach. In addition, periodic updates on international public sector standards and GASB standards will be provided to members.

Budget Resources

While the staff vacancies discussed above did not result from a direct reduction in budgetary resources, ongoing budget uncertainty – particularly resulting from the sequester – affected the timing of recruitment efforts and the ability to hire senior staff. As noted above, at year end, the assistant director vacancy was filled and planning was underway to fill the second vacancy.

Actual funding levels are dependent on final FY 2014 appropriations and will be determined after appropriations are provided to each of the board's sponsors. Table 1, *Budget 2011-2014*, presents budget resources used from FY 2011 through FY 2013 as well as anticipated resources for FY 2014.

Table 1: Budget 2011 – 2014 (dollars in thousands)				
	2011	2012	2013	Planned 2014
Salaries and Benefits	1,673.4	1,612.4	1,432.3	1,677.6
Member Compensation	153.5	149.0	148.6	152.7
Travel	61.7	48.0	41.3	52.0
Education & Training	16.0	10.8	14.0	10.8
Consultants and other	57.3	58.7	218.0 [2]	57.3
Total	**1,962.0**	**1,878.8**	**1,854.2**	**1,950.4**

[2] Note that contractor support was obtained in FY 2013 in light of staff vacancies.

Three-Year Plan for the Technical Agenda

The board prioritizes projects based on the following factors:

a) the likelihood a potential project will significantly contribute to meeting the operating performance and stewardship reporting objectives established in Statement of Federal Financial Accounting Concepts 1, *Objectives of Federal Financial Reporting*;

b) the significance of the issue relative to meeting reporting objectives;

c) the pervasiveness of the issue among federal entities; and

d) the potential project's technical outlook and resource needs.

Additional factors considered significant by individual members in planning the technical agenda include (1) a focus on citizens and citizen intermediaries as the primary users of the financial report of the U. S. government, (2) attention to the needs of Congress and program managers, (3) impacts on preparers and auditors due to declining real budgets, (4) increasing risks due to fiscal uncertainty and operational complexity, and (5) more electronic reporting.

With each annual review, the board identifies its priorities so that research can begin as time is available. Projects identified as priorities but not yet active on the board's agenda are "research projects." Your input regarding key issues and the scope of each research project is welcome.

This document presents the three-year plan in brief on page 11. A project plan for each active project follows. The board's research projects are then identified with a brief description. The final item in the technical agenda section is a list of potential projects considered by the board. You are welcome to submit suggestions on any aspect of this material or any ideas not presented herein.

If you have suggestions regarding the three-year plan, please submit them by email to: *fasab@fasab.gov*

or in hard copy to:

> Wendy M. Payne, Executive Director
> Federal Accounting Standards Advisory Board
> 441 G Street NW
> Suite 6814
> Washington, DC 20548

Table 2: Three-Year Plan in Brief

Project and Objective	FY 2013	FY 2014	FY 2015	FY 2016	FY 2017 – and Later
The Federal Reporting Entity: Consider what organizations and relationships should be included in federal entity reports and how information is to be presented	Issue Exposure Draft	Finalize Standards	Implementation Guidance as Needed		
Reporting Model: Consider whether the existing model meets user needs and reporting objectives Segments may include consideration of improvements in: - Cost information - Performance reporting - Budget presentation - Other areas such as the articulation of the financial statements	Develop Issues and Options	Consider results of Spending Pilots led by CFO Council Develop ideal model (concepts statement)	Finalize ideal model concepts statement in FY 2015 Identify discrete projects needed to support ideal model and decide vehicle(s) for guidance.		
Leases: Evaluate existing standards to improve comparability and completeness of reporting	Develop Exposure Draft	Issue Exposure Draft	Redeliberate and Finalize Standards		
Risk Assumed: Develop standards so that information about risks assumed by the federal government and their potential financial impacts are available		Issue Phase 1 Exposure Draft(s) Public Hearing Begin Phase II and III	Finalize Phase I Standards Develop Proposals for Phase II and III	Exposure Drafts for Phase II and III	Finalize Phases II and III Implementation Guidance as Needed
Public Private Partnerships: Consider how financial reporting objectives are met with regard to public private partnerships	Develop Project Plan and Begin Research	Develop and Issue Exposure Draft	Finalize Disclosure Standards and Develop Guidance in Recognition and Measurement Issues	Finalize recognition and measurement guidance	

Research Projects

Research projects are not assigned full-time staff but research may occur as resources become available. Projects are listed in order of priority. Anticipated date for assignment to staff indicated where possible.

Project and Objective	FY 2013	FY 2014	FY 2015	FY 2016	FY 2017 – and Later
Managerial Cost Accounting and Linking Cost to Performance (This project is related to the reporting model project. Decisions regarding next steps will be taken as the ideal model is developed.)		Independent Evaluation of User Needs for and Current State of Cost Accounting	Assign to staff depending on outcome of reporting model		
Tax Expenditures		Research			
Reconciling Budget and Accrual Information (This project is related to the reporting model project. Decisions regarding next steps will be taken as the ideal model is developed.)		Research	Assign to staff		
Natural Resources: Consider implementation guidance and recognition requirements for information reported during experimental period as Required Supplementary Information		Develop project plan and assign to staff	Begin Review to Reclassify Information		

Current Projects

The Federal Reporting Entity

Purpose: FASAB addresses the reporting entity issue in its Statement of Federal Financial Accounting Concepts (SFFAC) 2, *Entity and Display*. SFFAC 2 addresses:

- Reasons for Defining Reporting Entities
- Structure of the Federal Government
- Identifying the Reporting Entities for General Purpose Financial Reporting
- Criteria for Including Components in a Reporting Entity
- Other Issues Concerning the Completeness of the Entity

The board is aware of a number of entity issues. While SFFAC 2 provides criteria for determining if an entity should be included in the federal reporting entity, questions continue regarding whether certain organizations should be included. The Federal Reporting Entity project is addressing both the conceptual framework and standards issues. This phase will result in both proposed amendments to SFFAC 2 and one or more proposed standards.

Applicability: This project applies to the government-wide reporting entity and to component reporting entities that prepare and present general purpose federal financial reports in conformance with Statement of Federal Financial Accounting Standards (SFFAS) 34, *The Hierarchy of Generally Accepted Accounting Principles, Including the Application of Standards Issued by the Financial Accounting Standards Board.*

Objectives: To provide principles that guide preparers of financial statements in determining what organizations should be included in the financial reports of the government-wide reporting entity and each component reporting entity to meet federal financial reporting objectives.

Guide preparers of general purpose federal financial reports (GPFFR) in determining whether included entities are entities to be consolidated or entities to be disclosed, and what information should be presented. This guidance will ensure that users of GPFFR are provided with comprehensive financial information about entities and their involvements with organizations so that federal financial reporting objectives are met.

Develop a definition of 'related party' and establish relevant disclosure requirements.

Assigned staff: Melissa Loughan

Other resources: Staff has engaged a task force to help accomplish the project objectives.

Project page: *http://www.fasab.gov/projects/active-projects/concepts-federal-entity/*

Timeline: **August 2013 Meeting**
- Public hearing
- Discuss analysis of comments on ED and options for revising proposed standards

September 2013 to June 2014
- Draft Statement

June to August 2014
- Submit Statement to sponsors
- Issue Statement
- Consider the need for implementation guidance

Reporting Model

Purpose: This project is being undertaken by the board because of increased demands for financial information to facilitate decision-making and demonstrate accountability, and the changes in how users expect financial information to be delivered. For example, our research has noted that:
- Decision-makers are seeking information on the full cost of programs and citizens are accessing detailed information on spending, such as who received federal funds and what was accomplished with those funds. [3]
- Decision-makers also want additional information about the budget, comparisons of full costs with the budget, and projections of future receipts and expenditures.
- Citizens expect financial information about component entities but they have difficulty understanding current financial reports. [4]
- The public is relying increasingly on electronic media (digital devices, complex networks, and interactivity) to obtain information on demand. [5]

In addition, component entities are experimenting with a schedule of spending and the board may consider whether that schedule has a role as a basic financial statement. If so, guidance may be needed to help ensure that users understand the information presented and how it relates to existing financial statements.

Applicability: This project applies to the government-wide reporting entity and to component entities that prepare and present general purpose federal financial reports in conformance with

---

[3] Preparers Focus Group Discussion, February 10, 2009.
[4] FASAB, *User Needs Study: Citizens*, April 2010.
[5] FASAB Reporting Model Task Force, *Report to the FASAB*, December 22, 2010.

SFFAS 34, *The Hierarchy of Generally Accepted Accounting Principles, Including the Application of Standards Issued by the Financial Accounting Standards Board.*

Also, any conceptual guidance developed as a result of the project would guide the board's development of accounting and reporting standards. Knowledge of the concepts that the board considers should help users and others who are affected by or interested in federal financial accounting and reporting standards understand the purposes, content, and qualitative characteristics of information provided by federal financial accounting and reporting.

Objectives: The primary objectives of this project are to:

a. Determine what financial information would be helpful for decision-making, demonstrating accountability, and achieving the reporting objectives.

b. Determine how financial information should be presented to be most responsive to users and the manner in which they obtain information.

c. Consider how the information in a schedule of spending should relate to other financial statements and financial information presented in reports.

Assigned staff: Ross Simms

Other resources: Staff has been engaging a task force to help accomplish the project objectives. Also, staff plans to consider the schedule of spending pilot efforts. Optional resources include access to Web-based meeting software like Webex to reduce meeting logistics issues and permit wide participation.

Project page: *http://www.fasab.gov/projects/active-projects/concepts-the-financial-report/*

Timeline: **August – December 2013**
- Develop ideal model and draft concepts statement

January 2014 – June 2014 Meetings
- Review ED(s) or other proposals

August 2014 Meeting
- Issue ED(s) or other proposals for comment

October and December 2014 Meetings
- Discuss analysis of comments on ED(s) or other proposals

February and April 2015
- Draft Statement(s) or other guidance

May 2015
- Submit Statement(s) to sponsors or publish other guidance

July 2015
- Issue Statement(s) and decide on next steps to facilitate "ideal model"

Leases

Purpose: This project is being undertaken by the board primarily because the current lease accounting standards, SFFAS 5, *Accounting for Liabilities of the Federal Government*, and 6, *Accounting for Property, Plant, and Equipment*, have been criticized as ineffective because they do not make meaningful distinctions between capital and operating leases regarding the substance of lease transactions. In addition, the lease accounting standards in SFFAS 5 and 6 are based on Financial Accounting Standards Board (FASB) lease accounting standards which are currently being reviewed and are likely to be revised. The FASB and International Accounting Standards Board (IASB) have undertaken a joint project on lease accounting that focuses on the conveyance of rights to future economic benefits (such as the right of use). In addition, the Governmental Accounting Standards Board is undertaking a project to address lease standards. Staff of the two boards will collaborate in developing issues and options. Joint meetings of the boards will be held periodically to discuss options including differences between the state/local and federal environments.

Applicability: This project applies to the government-wide reporting entity and to component entities that prepare and present general purpose federal financial reports in conformance with SFFAS 34, *The Hierarchy of Generally Accepted Accounting Principles, Including the Application of Standards Issued by the Financial Accounting Standards Board.*

Objectives: The primary objectives of this project are to:

a. Develop an approach to lease accounting that would ensure that all assets and liabilities [consistent with SFFAC 5 definitions] arising under lease contracts are recognized in the statement of financial position and related costs are recognized in the statement of net cost.

b. Evaluate and revise as needed the current lease-related definitions and recognition guidance in SFFAS 5 and 6, including consideration of the advantages and disadvantages of applying the potential FASB/IASB lease standard in the federal environment.

c. Ensure that the standards to be developed fully address the various lease transactions/activities currently being used in the federal community (e.g. enhanced use leases).

d. Consider how the budgetary treatment of lease-purchases and leases of capital assets as outlined in Office of Management and Budget (OMB) Circular No. A-11 relates to financial statements and disclosures.

Assigned staff: Monica R. Valentine, Domenic Savini and incoming staff

Other resources: Staff will consult with both FASB and GASB staff members assigned to their board's respective lease accounting projects. Staff will also organize a task force of knowledgeable federal and non-federal participants who have relevant experience or interest in lease accounting within the federal government.

Project page: *http://www.fasab.gov/projects/active-projects/leases/*

Timeline: **September 2013 – August 2014**
- Work with task force and GASB staff to identify lease activities and lease accounting issues, including FASB/IASB proposal
- Present identified lease accounting issues for board consideration

October 2014 Meeting
- Review draft standards section

December 2014 Meeting
- Present first draft Exposure Draft (ED) for board review

February 2015 Meeting
- Issue ED

June – October 2015 Meetings
- Present initial analysis of ED comment letters received
- Conduct public hearing

December 2015 Meeting
- Discuss analysis of comments on ED

February – April 2016 Meetings
- Draft Statement
- Submit Statement(s) to sponsors

June – August 2016
- Issue Statement and decide next steps

Risk Assumed

Purpose:

This project is being undertaken by the board because existing FASAB standards on risk assumed are limited to insurance contracts and explicit guarantees (other than loan guarantees). Because the federal government has a variety of responsibilities and consequently assumes a range of risks, it is important that FASAB revisit its existing standards. For example, when implementing policy initiatives to stabilize financial markets and the economy, the federal government explicitly assumed risks previously considered by some to have implied backing of the federal government (GSE).

In order to meet the stewardship and operating performance objectives of federal financial reporting,[6] it is important that the federal government report all significant risks assumed, not just risks related to insurance contracts and explicit guarantees.

Applicability:

This project applies to the government-wide reporting entity and to component entities that prepare and present general purpose federal financial reports in conformance with SFFAS 34, *The Hierarchy of Generally Accepted Accounting Principles (GAAP), Including the Application of Standards Issued by the Financial Accounting Standards Board (FASB).*

Objectives:

The primary objective of this project is to study the significant risks assumed by the federal government and develop (a) definitions of risk assumed, (b) related recognition and measurement criteria, and (c) disclosure and / or required supplementary information (RSI) guidance that federal agencies can apply consistently in accordance with GAAP.

Assigned staff: Robin Gilliam and Monica Valentine

Other resources: Multi-disciplinary task force, including sub-groups to address specific topics.

Project page: *http://www.fasab.gov/projects/active-projects/risk-assumed/*

Timeline:

Phase I: Explicit Indemnification Arrangements (insurance and guarantees other than loans):
- Identify alternative measures of loss exposure (value at risk)
- Consider recognition of elements in accrual financial statements (measurement and recognition guidance)
- Consider needed disclosures and/or RSI

October 2013 – April 2014
- Begin identifying issues and drafting requirements

June – December 2014
- Issue ED or other request for feedback on Phase I
- Conduct pilot testing on Phase I
- Begin Phase II: Consider applicability to other types of risks assumed (entitlements other than social insurance, natural disasters, implicit or other explicit risks such as through governmental partnerships or treaties) and contingencies – follow steps

---

[6] SFFAC 1, *Objectives of Federal Financial Reporting*, pars. 100, 122, and 141

similar to Phase I but completion expected 18-24 months following completion of Phase I.

Febraury 2015
- Hold public hearing on Phase I

May – October 2015
- Finalize Phase I Statement
- Phase III: Consider implications for reporting on commitments (for example, is commitment reporting for grants, contracts, and other long-term agreements complete and consistent?)

December 2015
- Submit Phase I Statement

March 2016
- Issue Phase I Statement

2016 – 2017
- Develop implementation guidance for Phase I, if necessary
- Complete Phase II (entitlement programs, disaster response, regulatory activities, and interventions) and III (commitments and obligations arising from long-term contracts, treaties, and intergovernmental dependency) SFFASs

Public Private Partnerships

Purpose:	This project was added to the agenda because federal agencies have increasingly turned to public-private partnerships (e.g., PPPs, P3s) to accomplish goals. Budget pressures are likely to further increase the use of P3s. Making the full costs and risks of such partnerships transparent would be the overall objective of the project.

Specific objectives could include:
- Defining terms (e.g., service concession arrangements, P3s)
- Providing guidance for the recognition and measurement of:
    - assets and liabilities
    - revenues and expenses
    - risks
- Considering implications for other arrangements related to P3s (sale-leaseback or other long-term arrangements).

Applicability:	This project applies to the government-wide reporting entity and to component entities that prepare and present general purpose federal financial reports in conformance with SFFAS 34, *The Hierarchy of Generally Accepted Accounting Principles (GAAP), Including the Application of Standards Issued by the Financial Accounting Standards Board (FASB)*.
Objectives:	Because fairly robust FASAB guidance exists regarding the recognition and measurement of assets/liabilities and revenues/expenses, the primary objective of this project would be issue a Technical Bulletin providing guidance to resolve accounting issues not directly addressed by either the Statements or Interpretations. In addition, standards may be developed to require needed disclosure.
Assigned staff:	Domenic Savini

Other resources: After a brief initial research phase, staff plans to utilize a multi-disciplinary task force, including sub-groups to address specific topics.

Project page: *http://www.fasab.gov/projects/active-projects/public-private-partnerships/*

Timeline:

October – December 2013
- Present individual issues to task force and board

February 2014
- Develop and Issue Exposure Draft for additional disclosures

October 2014
- Finalize Guidance or Standards for additional disclosures

2015 – 2017
- Develop implementation guidance and/or standards in concert with leases and reporting entity projects

Research Projects

Managerial Cost Accounting and Linking Cost and Performance

The CFO Act calls for the development of cost information and the integration of accounting, program, and budget systems and information. Also, subsequent legislation such as the Government Performance and Results Act (GPRA) and Government Performance and Results Act Modernization Act established the expectation that cost measurement would be an important part of reporting on results. Accordingly, as illustrated in Figure 1: Role of Cost Data, cost data is vital to financial reporting, budget decision-making, and performance management and reporting and, ultimately, cost data is a key ingredient for fiscal management and demonstrating accountability.

Figure 1: Role of Cost Data

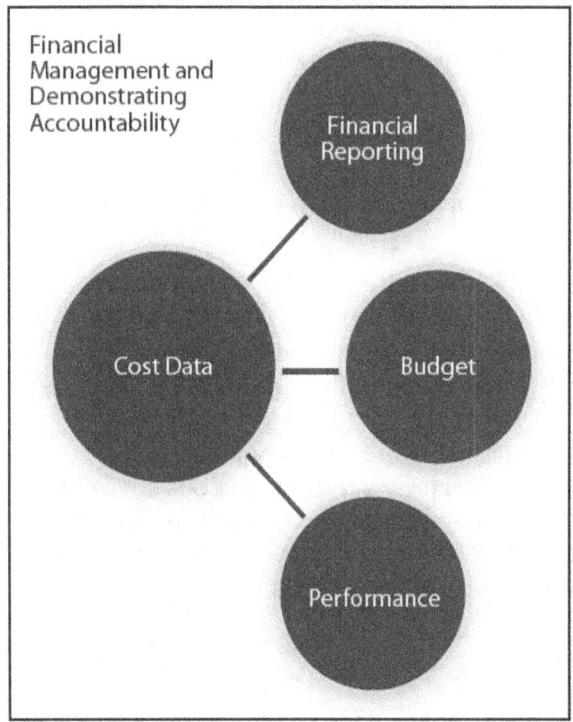

In 1995, to support the goals of the CFO Act and the GPRA, the board established managerial cost accounting standards. However, the board continues to be advised of a need to improve the internal availability of cost information and its linkage to performance information. In 2010, FASAB staff researched managerial cost accounting which included a survey of agencies. Results indicated that a guide to using, developing, and reporting cost information might be helpful. Also, research in the reporting model project identified cost accounting as critical to meeting a need to integrate cost, budget and other performance information. The ideal model under development in the reporting model project will inform this project regarding long-term goals for disaggregating and linking information.

The board is also undertaking a study, with the assistance of a contractor, that will support its development of a project plan. The study will address questions such as (1) are good financial and related data available to senior managers, (2) how effectively are managers using such data, (3) what gaps may exist, and (4) what options are most likely to be helpful in closing any gaps.

Given that cost data is central to integration and plays a significant role in financial management, a bottoms-up approach to the managerial cost accounting and linking cost and performance project could be considered. Under a bottoms-up approach, the objective would be to focus on helping to ensure that adequate, high-quality cost data is available to support integration and satisfy the range of user expectations. Adequate, high quality cost data could be classified, aggregated, and linked in various ways to provide the information that users expect and achieve the intent of the CFO Act and other legislation.

To facilitate appropriate consideration of significant issues, the project could be divided into segments. Each segment could be conducted by a task force which would provide its results to the board through FASAB staff. Figure 2: Potential Managerial Cost Accounting Segments briefly discusses potential segments.

Figure 2: Potential Managerial Cost Accounting Segments

Federal Managerial Cost Accounting

Elements

- Will help improve reporting cost and performance information and provide data for management decision-making

- Discusses the characteristics of cost accounting elements. Discussing the characteristics will help the community in consistently using the terminology and classifying costs for management and reporting purposes.

Measures

- Will help improve the information available for management decision-making.

- Discusses measures that would be useful for planning and controlling costs, financial reporting, and performance measurement

Presentation of Net Costs

- Will help improve reporting of cost and performance information and provide information for decision-making

- Provides requirements for classifying costs and determing when revenue items should be netted against costs or presented seperately

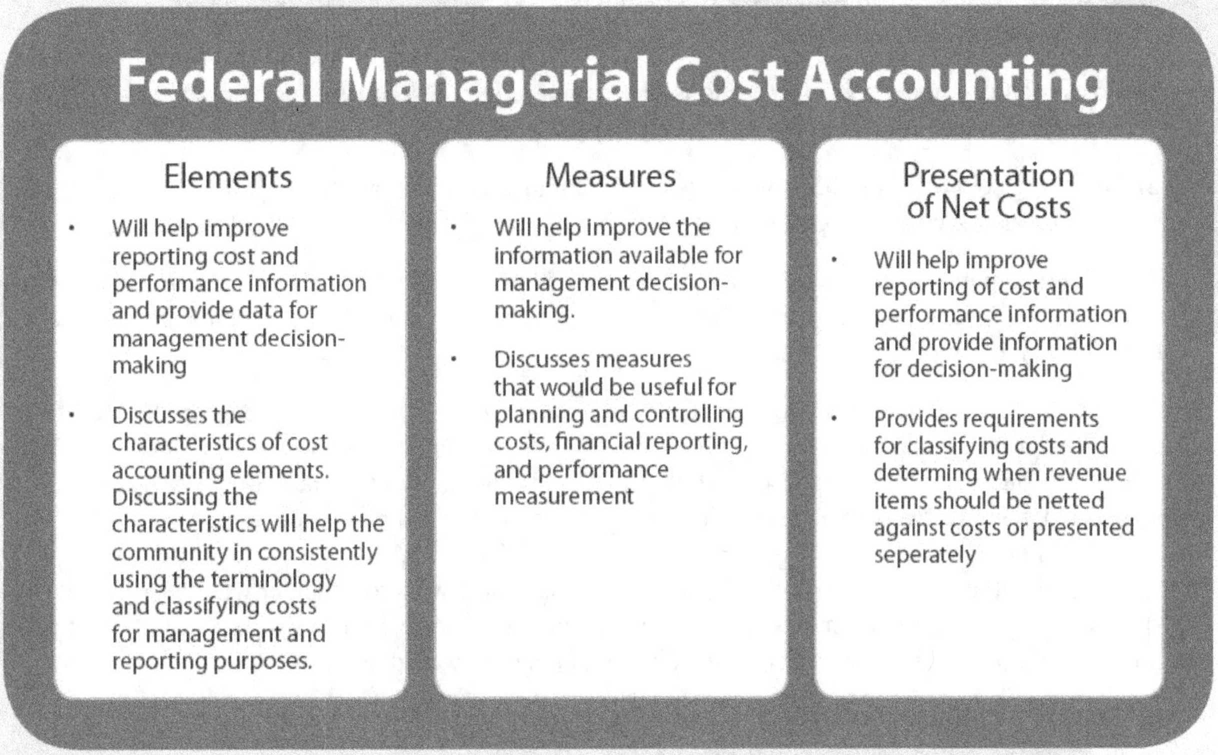

Knowing more about users' interest in cost information and preparers need for resources to guide development of cost information would be useful in planning this project. Comments regarding the scope and priorities of this project would be most welcome.

Reconciling Budget and Accrual Information

SFFAS 7, *Accounting for Revenue and Other Financing Sources and Concepts for Reconciling Budgetary and Financial Accounting*, requires information to explain the differences between budgetary and financial accounting information. The requirement results in a reconciliation of obligations incurred and net cost and is presented as a note.

The detailed provisions are:

80. Budgetary and financial accounting information are complementary, but both the types of information and the timing of their recognition are different, causing differences in the basis of accounting. To better understand these differences, a reconciliation should explain the relationship between budgetary resources obligated by the entity during the period and the net cost of operations. It should reference the reported "obligations incurred" and related adjustments as defined by OMB Circular A-34. It also should include other financing sources not included in "obligations incurred" such as imputed financing, transfers of assets, and donations of assets not included in budget receipts. [Text deleted by SFFAS No. 22] The total of these items comprises obligations and nonbudgetary resources.

81. This total should then be adjusted by:

(a) Resources that do not fund net cost of operations (e.g., changes in undelivered orders, appropriations received to pay for prior period costs, capitalized assets),

(b) Costs included in net cost of operations that do not require resources (e.g., depreciation and amortization expenses of assets previously capitalized), and

(c) Financing sources yet to be provided (those becoming available in future periods which will be used to finance costs recognized in determining net cost for the present reporting period).

82. The adjustments should be presented and explained in appropriate detail and in a manner that best clarifies the relationship between the obligations basis used in the budget and the accrual basis used in financial (proprietary) accounting.

A July 2012 AGA research report (Government-wide Financial Reporting) suggested improvements in process as well as standards. They stated "Our research indicated interest in the Unified Budget Deficit not only on the budgetary basis but also on the accrual basis and, more important, the reasons for the differences between the two perspectives." The government-wide financial report includes a basic financial statement reconciling the Unified Budget Deficit (deficit) and Net Cost. The deficit is based on receipts and outlays rather than obligations. So, the board may wish to consider whether revising the SFFAS 7, par. 80-82, requirements so that each component reporting entity reconciles net cost to amounts contributing to the government-wide deficit calculation would be:

1. An improvement in the information provided to users, and
2. Supportive of the government-wide reporting process improvements underway.

In contrast to the AGA report, many have suggested that the required reconciliation be eliminated while others recognize its usefulness (both as a control and as information helpful in understanding differences in perspectives). An effort to revise the reconciliation is likely to be controversial.

Input regarding user needs in this area and key questions from preparers and auditors would be helpful in planning this project. Your input would be most welcome.

Tax Expenditures

Presently, accounting standards do not require information regarding tax expenditures. SFFAS 7 provides that:

Information on tax expenditures that a reporting entity considers relevant to the performance of its programs may be presented, but should be qualified and explained appropriately to help the reader assess the possible impact of specific tax expenditures on the success of the related programs.

Tax expenditures are defined under the Congressional Budget and Impoundment Control Act of 1974, as amended, (the "Budget Act") as "revenue losses attributable to provisions of the Federal tax laws which allow a special exclusion, exemption, or deduction from gross income or which provide a special credit, a preferential rate of tax, or a deferral of tax liability." Thus, tax expenditures include any reductions in income tax liabilities that result from special tax provisions or regulations that provide tax benefits to particular taxpayers. Special income tax provisions are referred to as tax expenditures because they may be considered to be analogous to direct outlay programs, and the two can be considered as alternative means of accomplishing similar budget policy objectives. Tax expenditures are similar to those direct spending programs that are available as entitlements to those who meet the statutory criteria established for the programs. Tax expenditure analysis can help both policymakers and the public to understand the actual size of government, the uses to which government resources are put, and the tax and economic policy consequences that follow from the implicit or explicit choices made in fashioning legislation. (Source: Joint Committee on Taxation, Report JCX-15-11, March 9, 2011)

For FY 2012, estimates of tax expenditures are $1,092.5 billion while tax revenues are $1,912.5 billion. (Source: Pew Charitable Trusts at http://subsidyscope.org/tax_expenditures/summary/ - accessed April 10, 2013)

Growth in tax expenditures has been significant since SFFAS 7 first addressed the issue.

For FY 2013, The following chart shows the growth in tax expenditures from 2000 through 2015 (estimated) based on Treasury estimates:

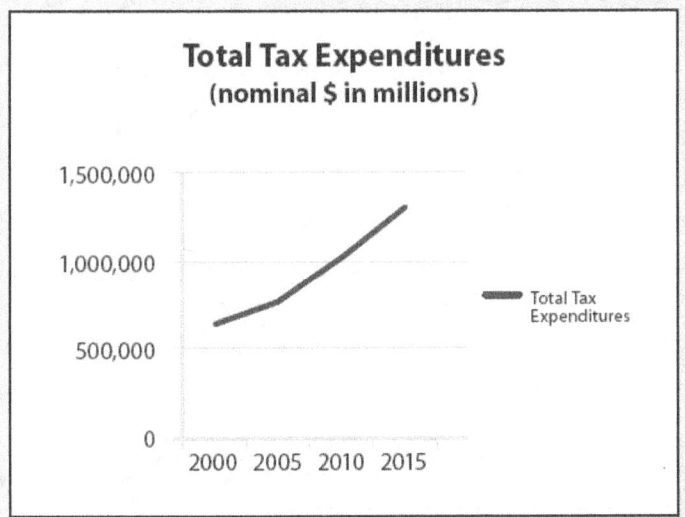

Tax expenditure information is also available by budget function. In some cases, tax expenditures are significant when considered in comparison to direct spending (outlays) for a particular budget function. Absent information about tax expenditures, it may be difficult to assess the full cost of government actions.

In planning this project, it would be helpful to hear from users about the information they would find most useful and any challenges they anticipate in communicating information on this complex topic. Your input would be most welcome.

Natural Resources

SFFAS 38, *Accounting for Federal Oil and Gas Resources*, was issued as final on April 13, 2010. It requires the value of the federal government's estimated petroleum royalties from the production of federal oil and gas proved reserves to be reported in a schedule of estimated federal oil and gas petroleum royalties. In addition, it requires the value of estimated petroleum royalty revenue designated for others to be reported in a schedule of estimated federal oil and gas petroleum royalties to be distributed to others. These schedules are to be presented in required supplementary information (RSI) as part of a discussion of all significant federal oil and gas resources under management by the entity. Due to a deferral (SFFAS 41), the Statement is effective as RSI for periods beginning after September 30, 2012.

It is the board's intent that the information required by the Statement transition to basic information after being reported as RSI for a period of three years. Prior to the conclusion of the three-year RSI period, the board plans to decide whether such information should be recognized in the financial statements or disclosed in notes. This Statement will remain in effect until such time a determination is made.

The purpose of this project is to consider the results of the three-year RSI period and develop standards regarding any transition of information to basic information.

Potential Projects

After considering factors that may influence project priorities, the board begins its planning by reviewing potential projects identified by the Executive Director (see Figure 1 for the rules of procedure governing agenda setting). Note that the list accumulates over time. Generally, potential projects are only removed if the issue has clearly been addressed through other projects.

Stakeholders are encouraged to contact the Executive Director to suggest potential projects or to provide insight regarding the projects identified here. Instructions for submitting comments are presented on page 35.

Index of Potential Projects

Rules of Procedure
Regarding Agenda Setting

The FASAB consults with the Executive Director to prioritize its potential projects. New projects are added to the active agenda based on periodic prioritization by the board. The Executive Director ensures that agenda decisions are initiated in advance of staff becoming available to take on new work so that pre-agenda research will be conducted. All agenda decisions are made at meetings of the FASAB by oral polling with agreement of at least a majority of members polled required for approval.

To prepare for the FASAB consultation, the Executive Director solicits timely suggestions from other individuals and organizations. The Executive Director, after consultation with the Chairperson, may publish brief descriptions of potential projects and request input from selected individuals and groups on the potential projects and other emerging issues. In addition, the Chairperson may decide to convene an agenda hearing to discuss potential projects with stakeholders.

In addition to agenda setting initiated by FASAB, any individual or organization may request in writing or at an open meeting that the FASAB address a new issue, or review or reexamine any effective Statement of Federal Financial Accounting Standards, Statement of Federal Financial Accounting Concepts, or other effective provision of federal accounting principles. The FASAB will respond to such communications and explain its disposition of the request.

Asset Retirement Obligations

In some circumstances entities may be required to incur costs to retire assets. The board has established general standards for liability recognition and specific standards for liabilities associated with environmental cleanup (in SFFAS 5, *Accounting for Liabilities of the Federal Government*, and SFFAS 6, *Accounting for Property, Plant and Equipment*, respectively). However, there is no specific guidance regarding asset retirement obligations other than cleanup costs (e.g., hazardous materials required by law to be cleaned up). GAAP for the private sector includes specific guidance regarding asset retirement obligations developed since issuance of SFFAS 6. Financial Accounting Standards Statement No. 143, *Accounting for Asset*

Retirement Obligations (issued 6/01) requires that the fair value of a liability for an asset retirement obligation be recognized in the period in which it is incurred if a reasonable estimate of fair value can be made. The associated asset retirement costs are capitalized as part of the carrying amount of the long-lived asset. This creates three inconsistencies between entities following federal GAAP and those following FASB GAAP. One, certain liabilities recognized under FASB standards would not be recognized in the federal sector. Two, FASB standards require that liabilities be recognized in full when the obligation occurs while FASAB standards provide for incremental recognition so that the full liability is recognized at the end of the useful life of the asset requiring environmental cleanup. Three, the asset retirement costs are added to the total cost of the asset under FASB standards and are not in the federal sector; instead these costs are expensed as the liability is recognized.

Cleanup Costs – Evaluating Existing Standards

SFFAS 6, *Accounting for Property, Plant and Equipment*, addresses cleanup costs. Issues regarding existing standards for cleanup costs include:

1. Whether the existing liability recognition provisions are consistent with element definitions established in SFFAC 5.

    a) The liability may be understated because the obligation is to clean up the entire hazardous waste but SFFAS 6 provides for a gradual build up of the liability balance as the related PP&E is consumed in service (the full cleanup cost is disclosed in a note).

    b) The cost of PP&E may be understated because the SFFAS 6 requirement is to capitalize its acquisition cost; the later cost to retire the asset is excluded.

    c) The scope of liability recognition is limited to costs to clean up hazardous substances rather than the full asset retirement obligation.

2. Cost-benefit issues relating to the level of precision required for estimates and ongoing concerns regarding the timing of recognition of asbestos liabilities (generally when asbestos exists rather than when it is to be removed) have been raised.

Conceptual Framework – Review and Finalization

The board undertook a project to refresh and complete its conceptual framework. Work began in 2006 and the stated objectives were a framework to:

*   provide structure by describing the nature and limits of federal financial reporting including the boundaries of the federal reporting entity,

*   identify objectives that give direction to standard setters,

*   define the elements critical to meeting financial reporting objectives and describe the statements used to present elements,

*   identify means of communicating information necessary to meeting objectives and describe when a particular means should be used, and

*   enable those affected by or interested in standards to understand better the purposes, content, and characteristics of information provided in federal financial reports.

The board established a phased approach and in the case of the reporting entity phase the effort led to development of standards concurrent with amendments to existing concepts. The board envisioned a final review of the resulting concepts to ensure consistency across the framework and to confirm its completeness. The board completed new concepts on elements of accrual bases financial statements and measurement of those elements as well as placement of information (basic, RSI and OAI).

During the project, other standards-setting bodies, including GASB, FASB, IASB and the IPSASB, undertook similar efforts. Some of their efforts will go farther than the board's. For example, the FASB is considering a disclosure framework and the IASB is discussing principles for selecting among measurement approaches (e.g., relevance, giving priority to how the measurement approach affects the statement of comprehensive income, and cost-benefit). Coverage of topics by these standards-setting bodies may be more comprehensive than the board's coverage and the board may benefit from considering their efforts.

If this project were undertaken, the board would review its framework (including the results of the reporting entity and reporting model projects) and ensure the framework is complete and internally consistent.

Cost of Capital

The opportunity cost of making an investment in assets is not recognized in the financial statements of agencies using the assets. Some other national governments have incorporated a capital use charge into the determination of the cost of agency operations as a management tool. The board considered this issue in connection with SFFAS 6 and issued an invitation to comment. Ultimately the board deferred further work on this project. In doing so, the board noted that there was interest in incorporating a cost of capital in the budget and that progress in this area would benefit the board's work. If this project were undertaken, the board would need to consider the likely effectiveness of incorporating a capital charge in agency financial statements, the appropriate capital base on which to assess the charge, and the selection of an interest rate to apply.

Derivatives

Staff has not researched the use of derivatives by federal agencies and has not had any inquiries by agencies or their auditors regarding appropriate accounting for derivatives. This is an area generally addressed in other domains. [7] The GASB issued Statement No 64, *Derivative Instruments: Application of Hedge Accounting Termination Provisions, an amendment of GASB Statement No. 53*, on the topic. Selected material from the GASB's plain language explanation is presented below.

What is a Derivative?

A derivative is a unique and often complex financial arrangement that a government may enter into with another party, typically a private-sector financial firm. The value of a derivative or the cash it provides to a government (or that it requires a government to pay) is based on changes in the market prices of an item that is being hedged, such as interest rates on long term bonds or commodity prices. In other words, the value or cash flows of a derivative are derived from (are determined by) how the market prices of the hedged item change.

Governments enter into derivatives for at least four reasons:

- Governments often intend derivatives to be hedges. This type of derivative is an attempt to significantly reduce a specific financial risk that a government identifies, such as the risk of increasing commodity costs.

- Some governments find that they can lower their borrowing costs by entering into a derivative in connection with debt they issue.

---

[7] Presently, derivatives are reported in federal financial reports in conformance with private-sector standards.

- Some governments engage in derivatives that are investments—governments are trying to generate income, as they would by buying other financial instruments.

- Some governments enter into derivatives to manage their cash flows. These derivatives may include an up-front cash payment to the government from the other party. The payment arrangements or terms of the derivative agreement essentially provide for the repayment of the up-front cash.

Electromagnetic Spectrum

The Federal Communications Commission (FCC) manages the electromagnetic spectrum – a renewable natural resource excluded from coverage in Technical Bulletin 2011-1. The technical bulletin requires entities to report the federal government's estimated royalties and other revenue from federal natural resources that are (1) under lease, contract or other long-term agreement and (2) reasonably estimable as of the reporting date in required supplementary information.

The FCC's goal is to:

Ensure efficient allocation and management of assets that government controls or influences, such as spectrum, poles, and rights-of-way, to encourage network upgrades and competitive entry.

This project would consider what information may be needed to allow citizens to monitor the management of this asset. It is not addressed by other accounting standards at this time. Based on the Fiscal Year 2013 Budget Estimates submitted by the FCC to Congress in February 2012, receipts in excess of $30 billion are anticipated over the next ten years.

Excerpt from Congressional Research Service Report: Spectrum Policy in the Age of Broadband: Issues for Congress (Linda K. Moore, Specialist in Telecommunications Policy, August 29, 2012 (R40674))

Electronic Reporting

Electronic reporting is increasingly viewed as a means to convey financial information about government. This is evidenced not only by sites such as USAspending.gov and Recovery.gov but also by the universal practice of posting annual financial reports to federal websites and the emerging practice of providing a written highlights document accompanied by an electronic copy of the full report. More recently, a requirement that performance reports be provided electronically rather than in printed form was established in law (GPRAMA). In addition, there is a growing expectation that machine readable data be provided. This is an area of great interest to the profession and the Association of Government Accountants issued Research Series Report No. 32 on e-Reporting in July 2012. The full report is available at *http://www. agacgfm.org/Research-(1)/Research-Publications.aspx*. The AGA report revealed a desire for common definitions, formats, and content among survey participants. Useful information regarding desired reporting and the need for standards and/or best practice guidance was provided through the research report.

The AGA report recommends, among other actions, the following actions relevant to standards-setting:

1. "An organization, group or taskforce of stakeholders should be appointed from the standard-setting community, federal, state and local government preparers, representatives from various public interest groups, and citizen-users — all with the collective charge to develop guidelines through an open dialogue and with a shared vision for data formatting and common reporting. This group should also encourage the discovery and recommendation of and reward for best practices in government financial, non-financial and performance information reporting."

2. The above group should "set definitions and strategies and create uniform standards for data content, database design and logical data model constructs for easier extraction, transformation and processing. Integrating federal, state and local information is critical. Standardization must be stable and able to survive challenges from preparers, data providers, systems vendors and users among others who are wedded to their existing systems and approaches." [8]

A summary of the concerns/practices that might be addressed through guidelines – perhaps as recommended practices – follows and matters of particular relevance to FASAB are underlined. [9]

1) Should financial information be complete even when reported electronically?

    a) <u>How might boundaries and completeness of an electronic report be made clear to the user?</u>

        i) A warning message showing when you are leaving the financial report

        ii) Information regarding the contents and structure of a generally accepted accounting principles (GAAP) basis financial report should be provided when GAAP basis financial reports are accessed

    b) Should information provided outside of the GAAP basis financial report be clearly marked as such and any departure from the principles established for the financial report disclosed?

        i) <u>Any excerpts from a GAAP basis financial report might provide a reference to the complete financial report.</u>

        ii) <u>Accounting principles might be explained (whether GAAP or another basis) and linked to discrete items of information including disclosures (e.g., if a line item is accessed, an explanation of the accounting policies related to the line item as well as any related disclosure can be easily accessed).</u>

    c) <u>Whether financial information presented on a web page is audited should be noted.</u>

    d) Should electronic reporting beyond GAAP basis financial reports supplement or complement these reports?

        i) Explanations of differences in principles should be provided.

        ii) Non-GAAP basis pages should include a link to GAAP basis financial reports.

2) Should Web pages be clearly dated and timely?

3) Communication with users (Interactive websites)

    a) <u>Are financial terms adequately defined and appropriately used on websites?</u>

    b) Is adequate announcement of the availability of electronic financial reports made?

    c) Can financial reports be easily located?

        i) Search features may need to be enhanced to help users locate the e-report

        ii) A common "portal" to access all financial reports may be useful. For example, the Financial Report of the US Government could serve as the portal to component reports.

    d) Automated e-mail alerts to interested users

    e) A single point of contact at each entity to respond to questions

    f) What constitutes good practice regarding posting of relevant links for the interested user? (considering both benefits and drawbacks of links)

---

[8] Association of Government Accountants, *e-Reporting*, July 2012, pages 20-21.

[9] Note that it is not suggested that each of these is a matter of concern that FASAB should address through standards. For example, some members suggested educational materials such as best practices.

    g) Many technology related issues emerge such as

        i) Speed of download

        ii) Use of pictures (thumbnails)

        iii) When should "plug-ins" be used?

4) Accessibility issues to consider include:

    a) Is the data downloadable to facilitate analysis?

    b) Are appropriate historical data available?

    c) Are internal and external links maintained (no broken links)?

5) Are security/control measures adequate?

    a) Process of posting data prevents errors

    b) Appropriate authorization to edit data

    c) Controls to prevent unauthorized access (both internally and externally)

    d) Hyperlinks to unaudited data – is adequate disclosure in place and does security extend to the unaudited data? Is the user able to differentiate between complete and incomplete data?

    e) Auditor relationship with electronically published data

        i) Relationship with existing GAAP based financial reports

        ii) Assurance over real-time electronic reporting?

    f) Quality assurance over unaudited data

        i) Source of data (e.g., financial systems, procurement data base, cuff records)

        ii) Controls

        iii) Reconciliation to other data sources

Sources:

Iqbal Khadaroo. (2005). Corporate reporting on the internet: some implications for the auditing profession. *Managerial Auditing Journal*, 20(6), 578-591.

Arumugam Seetharaman, Ramaiyer Subramaniam, & Seow Yuan Shyong. (2005). Internet Financial Reporting: Problems and Prospects (PART II). *Corporate Finance Review*, 10(2), 23-34.

D, Hurburgh. (2000). The Web: Where financial information belongs. *JASSA*, (2), 16-20.

Richard Fisher, Peter Oyelere, & Fawzi Laswad. (2004). Corporate reporting on the Internet: Audit issues and content analysis of practices. *Managerial Auditing Journal*, 19(3), 412-439.

Barry Smith. (2005) An Investigation of the Integrity of Internet Financial Reporting. *The International Journal of Digital Accounting Research*, 5(9), 47-48.

Evaluating Existing Standards

A general concern expressed by members of the board and the federal financial management community has been that resources are increasingly constrained. Because of competing demands, existing requirements should be evaluated and any unnecessary requirements eliminated. This has been a long-standing concern that the board considers carefully in existing projects.

To explore burden reduction in a targeted fashion, project objectives could include:

1. provide forums for preparers, auditors, and users to identify requirements they believe are unnecessary (this could be done through an open-ended written request for input or roundtable discussions)

2. evaluate the requirements identified against the reporting objectives

3. prepare an omnibus exposure draft to adjust or eliminate requirements

The challenge in this approach is that the relevance of requirements varies among agencies. For example, agencies for which certain requirements are immaterial may not find the information relevant but may find the steps necessary to omit the required information based on materiality too burdensome. They may simply comply with the requirement. To reduce the burden on this agency would mean that the requirement also would be eliminated at an agency for which the information is material. In addition, the burden is likely different between agencies with and without strong systems and controls.

Financial/Economic Condition

The board provided standards regarding fiscal sustainability reporting. However, a broader focus on financial condition reporting might result in additional reporting such as key indicators of financial condition at the agency or government-wide level. GASB has addressed key indicators and is currently undertaking a project to address financial projections.

Questions such as the following could be addressed in the project:

- What key financial ratios are useful in assessing the financial health of the entity?
- What information about the tax system is viewed as an indicator of financial health? (e.g., tax gap, tax expenditures, changes in the tax base/structure)
- Is cost trend information needed at disaggregated levels? (e.g., trends in construction costs for capital intensive operations or personnel costs for labor intensive operations)
- Are there external reports/measures that should be reported such as rating agency reports regarding sovereign nations?
- Are benchmarks against other nations/departments needed?
- Are measures of risk assumed due to inter-governmental financial dependency needed?

Intangibles

The FASAB standards do not address intangible assets other than internal use software. Staff has been contacted by a few individuals with respect to intangibles such as census data and rights to use of inventions. The GASB issued *Accounting and Financial Reporting for Intangible Assets*. The issuance is described as follows on the GASB website:

Statement No. 51 identifies an intangible asset as having the following three required characteristics:

- It lacks physical substance—in other words, you cannot touch it, except in cases where the intangible is carried on a tangible item (for example, software on a DVD).
- It is nonfinancial in nature—that is, it has value, but is not in a monetary form like cash or securities, nor is it a claim or right to assets in a monetary form like receivables, nor a prepayment for goods or services.
- Its initial useful life extends beyond a single reporting period.

The standard generally requires intangible assets to be treated as capital assets, following existing authoritative guidance for capital assets, although certain intangible assets are specifically excluded from the scope of the statement. One key exclusion relates to intangible assets that are acquired or created primarily for the purpose of directly obtaining income or profit. Such intangible assets should be treated as investments. The standard also provides guidance for issues specific to intangible assets. For instance, to report the historical cost of an intangible asset in the financial statements, the asset has to be *identifiable*. That means that the asset is *separable*—the government can sell, rent, or otherwise transfer it to another party. If it is not separable, the asset has to arise from contractual or other legal rights, such as water rights acquired from another government through a contract that cannot be transferred to another party.

Internal Use Software

SFFAS 10 provides standards for internal use software. Since its implementation, federal preparers have expressed concerns regarding (1) the relevance of capitalized costs which are limited to the development phase (both OMB guidance and GAO's cost estimating guide focus broadly on project – or life-cycle – costs), (2) the need to assign full costs – which include general and administrative costs – to software, and (3) the ability to identify phases under current IT practices. The objectives of the project would be to:

- Evaluate whether restricting capitalized costs to the development phases is useful and, if not, consider changes such as allowing capitalization from project inception to completion or expensing costs.
- Consider alternatives to the current full cost requirements and/or guidance to support efficient agency implementation.

Long-Term Construction/Development/Procurement Contracts

In its work on National Defense PP&E (ND PP&E), the board considered the need for disclosures regarding complex, long duration contracts for the development and acquisition of weapons systems. One proposal included a disclosure of the ten largest acquisition programs showing budgeted amounts, expected amounts, cost to date and progress to date. Exposure of this proposed disclosure requirement revealed a number of technical areas that required clarification as well as resistance to this non-traditional disclosure among some commentators. The board elected to move forward to eliminate the special category ND PP&E and any disclosures unique to the category. As a result, the board set aside its work in this area. However, the board noted (in the Basis for Conclusions to a subsequent ED and SFFAS 23 – *Eliminating the Category National Defense PP&E*) its intention to return to this proposal on a government-wide basis in the future.

Omnibus AICPA

The initial objective of the project was to consider incorporating accounting and financial reporting standards that are included in current and recently modified Statements on Auditing Standards (SASs) to more effectively present those standards so that these requirements become the responsibility of the financial statement preparers. The scope included analysis of current and recently modified SASs to identify accounting and financial reporting standards. The board then analyzed that guidance to determine if that guidance should be incorporated into the FASAB literature.

The primary research issue is identifying, in the SASs, the various accounting and financial reporting requirements. Of the topics initially identified, the following topics have been addressed:

1) Hierarchy of generally accepted accounting principles

2) Subsequent events requirements

The board is currently addressing related party transactions in its project on the federal reporting entity.

These topics have not yet been addressed and are not within the scope of another project:

3) Materiality consideration (rollover versus iron curtain approaches) [10]

4) Going concern

At this time, the board does not anticipate resuming work on the project in the near future.

Property with Reversionary Interest

The federal government sometimes retains an interest in PP&E acquired by grantees with grant money. In the event that the grant recipient no longer uses the PP&E in the activity for which the grant was provided, the PP&E reverts to the federal government. These arrangements are specifically excluded from PP&E accounting. Some have suggested that a review of this exclusion is needed to ensure that similar arrangements are accounted for similarly and that adequate information is reported in such circumstances.

Research and Development

Research and development (R&D) costs are presented as required supplementary stewardship information (RSSI) and include both direct R&D spending by agencies and spending which supports non-federal research and development. Generally, staff has found that FASB standards for R&D are referenced to determine what spending qualifies as R&D (for example, to identify when to begin capitalizing costs as new assets are developed). Given the significant federal investment in R&D ($130.3 billion in 2012 [11]) and the possible differences between sectors, a review of practices in this area may be warranted. Alternatively, R&D reporting may be explored as a component of an overall project focusing on Stewardship Investments.

Revenue (Exchange and NonExchange)

SFFAS 7, *Accounting for Revenue and Other Financing Sources and Concepts for Reconciling Budgetary and Financial Accounting*, provides guidance for recognition of exchange and non-exchange revenue. In FY 2012, $350.8 billion of exchange revenue and $2,518.2 billion of non-exchange revenue was reported government-wide. SFFAS 7 requires disclosures and required supplementary information as well as suggests other accompanying information on the following topics:

*   A perspective on the income tax burden.

*   Available information on the size of the tax gap.

*   Tax expenditures related to entity programs.

*   Directed flows of resources related to entity programs.

---

[10] The rollover approach quantifies a misstatement based on the amount of the error originating in the current year income statement. It ignores the effects of correcting the portion of the current year balance sheet misstatement that originated in prior years (i.e., it ignores the "carryover effects" of prior year misstatements). The iron curtain approach quantifies a misstatement based on the effects of correcting the misstatement existing in the balance sheet at the end of the current year, irrespective of the misstatement's year(s) of origination. (Adapted from Securities and Exchange Commission Staff Accounting Bulletin 108)

[11] Consolidated Financial Report of the U. S. Government, FY 2012, Table 11.

SFFAS 7 has not been reviewed. Feedback suggests that some agencies are relying on FASB standards for more detailed guidance regarding revenue recognition and these standards are expected to be revised soon. When SFFAS 7 was established, the board acknowledged both inherent and practical limitations that made full accrual accounting for tax revenues unattainable. The basis for conclusions for SFFAS 7 notes:

> 171. At the time the Board began deliberations on this standard, accounting systems necessary to determine even the limited revenue accruals that are now required for taxes did not exist. The changes in systems required by this standard are limited to those necessary to mirror the established assessment processes. The Board understands that the Internal Revenue Service is attempting to improve its collection function and the related management information systems. Because such systems must also provide accounting information, the Board decided not to impose accounting standards at this time that might conflict with systems changes needed to improve the efficiency and effectiveness of the collection process or go beyond the minimum changes considered necessary to enable the collecting entities to properly discharge their responsibilities.

> 173. In the future, the general standard for accrual as it applies to taxes and duties could be tightened to produce a fuller application of the accrual concept. For fines, penalties and donations, no accountable event precedes the recognition point established by this standard. Therefore, the general standard for recognition as it applies to these sources of revenue results in full accrual accounting for them.

A review of the revenue standards might consider general improvements that could better meet the reporting objectives as well as how to improve the understandability of the presentation of information about taxes.

Statement of Changes in Cash

The Association of Government Accountants Research Report No. 31, *Government-wide Financial Reporting* (July 2012), recommended that the statement of changes in cash be modified to include information on (1) cash flow from operations, (2) debt financing activities and (3) investing activities. The report indicated that information regarding cash flows and whether the Treasury can fund operations within the operating cycle merits disclosure. Further, they found that "information on gross cash flows related to such matters as the making and collection of direct loans, purchase and disposal of investments (including activities to stabilize the economy) and flows needed to fund ongoing deficits is important to allow users to put results in perspective and understand future financing needs." The recommendations also include consideration of the status of this statement as basic or required supplementary information.

Stewardship Investments

The board undertook the effort to reclassify all required supplementary stewardship information (RSSI) several years ago. RSSI is not a category recognized in auditing standards. Audit coverage of the information may not meet the board's expectations unless the board reclassifies the information in an established category. Hence, the reclassification would resolve questions regarding the desired audit status of the information. The board completed work on two of three types of information – stewardship responsibilities and stewardship property, plant and equipment. The remaining RSSI type is stewardship investments including human capital, research and development, and non-federal physical property. The board deferred addressing this type so that it could devote additional resources to higher priority projects. The consequence is that this information remains as required supplementary information.

Summary or Popular Reporting

Agencies are issuing summary reports of financial and performance information and some view these as the primary report for citizen users. The need for guidance or standards has not been explored by staff. However, citizens participating in focus groups provided valuable insights regarding their interests and expectations.

Support and Outreach through Guidance and Education

While this item would best be considered in the context of strategic planning, it is listed here as a reminder of alternatives other than addition of major technical projects. Staff provides advice to preparers and auditors on an informal basis and supports education through review of textbooks, public speaking and other educational avenues (such as the CGFM program). Allocation of additional resources to this area might include (1) development of user guides, (2) more formal implementation guidance, or (3) evaluation of user needs and focus groups on communicating effectively through financial reports.

(This page intentionally left blank)

We want to hear from you.
Do you like this report? Do you believe it should include any other information?
Please let us know by contacting the Chairman at *FASAB@FASAB.GOV* or 202.512.7350.

FASAB Staff

Wendy Payne, Executive Director	202.512.7357	*paynew@fasab.gov*
Terri Pinkney, Executive Assistant	202 512-7350	*pinkneyt@fasab.gov*
Charles Jackson, Administrative Officer	202 512-7352	*jacksoncw1@fasab.gov*
Robin Gilliam, Assistant Director	202 512-7356	*gilliamr@fasab.gov*
Melissa Loughan, Assistant Director	202 512-5976	*loughanm@fasab.gov*
Domenic Savini, Assistant Director	202 512-6841	*savinid@fasab.gov*
Ross Simms, Assistant Director	202 512-2512	*simmsr@fasab.gov*
Monica Valentine, Assistant Director	202 512-7362	*valentinem@fasab.gov*

www.ingramcontent.com/pod-product-compliance
Lightning Source LLC
Chambersburg PA
CBHW080635290526
45790CB00007B/3078